Five Years In The Fog

Overcoming Obstacles

By Author Tracy Tate-Jones

COPYRIGHT by Tracy Tate Jones

All rights reserved. No part of this book may be reproduced or transmitted in any form or by any means, electronic or mechanical, except for permitted in Section 107 or 108 of the 1976 United States Copyright Act, without prior written consent of the publisher except for the inclusion of brief quotes in a review. While the author and the publisher have used their best efforts in preparing this book, they make no representations or warranties with respect to the accuracy or completeness of the contents of this book.

Published by Write It Away Publishing (Shamay Speaks)
www.WriteItAwayPublishing.com

Book cover designed by Shauny B Smith (KnockSmith Productions)
www.KnocksmithMagazine.com

Printed in the United States of America

ISBN: 978-0-9966729-6-2

Professionally edited by: Dayna Plummer

Synopsis

Five Years in a Fog, Overcoming Obstacles is the follow up book to my chapter **From the Frying Pan into the Fire** in the book **Broken Into Brilliance Vol. II,** presented by Tanicia Shamay Speaks Currie. In that chapter the story of survival, broken trust, abuse and abandonment was presented. Have you ever felt like you are the only person going through trials and tribulations or have asked the infamous question **WHY ME**? Well you are not alone. **Five Years in a Fog, Overcoming Obstacles** is a motivational book inspired by events that happened in my life that required me to overcome the hurt, shame, embarrassment, and grief to find peace within. Day after day, there's always something. This is a masterpiece detailing the trials and triumphs of events that overpowered my life. The story tells my truths to give motivation, encouragement and an inspirational blue print for those who have suffered or are suffering from trials and tribulations. This is a story of triumph over my shattered pieces of life from abuse, loss, addiction and fear that led me to compromise my true values to drown out my brokenness. There are many times in life that one must self-evaluate to find the answers to choices, desires, addictions, grief and fears. Looking within must become an automatic process in order to triumph over those trials one endures. I had to look within for the strength, courage and motivation to share my story. My story of survival and endurance changed the outlook of my life to find a peace within. I am blessed to be a blessing to others.

Table of Contents

Dedication/Acknowledgement vii

Introduction 1

Year 1_In the Frying Pan; One Tragedy to the Next 7

Year 2_In the Fire; What Knight? 17

Year 3 _ Homelessness; Everything Lost 25

Year 4_ Lost in Addiction 31

Year 5_ Failed Recovery 37

Successful Recovery 43

Giving Back; Beat the Streets, Inc. 51

The Triumph 58

About the Author 61

Dedication/Acknowledgement

I am dedicating this book to my son, Domonic White, first and foremost. He's been on this journey with me through thick and thin, since the beginning. He has been my rock and encourager to not only tell my truth, but his too. I would like to say I love you to infinity, I'm proud of you, and the best is yet to come. In your dedication I include my first granddaughter Na'ilah. I love you as my own and will leave a legacy for you if it's the last thing I do.

To my husband, Donald Jones, thank you for being a part of the foundation of my recovery. You have always encouraged me, even in silence. You've endured long days and long nights of me being in my own world, then and now. Thank you from the bottom of my heart. In your dedication, I include our daughters, Brianna, Deanna and Jaianna. You girls came into my life at the right time and allowed me to be your step-mother. That responsibility was an honor and our bond is unbreakable. I love you as my own, as well as your children. I am Granny.

An honorable mention to my publisher, Tanicia Shamay Speaks Currie, your vision allowed me to share my story of triumph and to come out of the shade with confidence. Your direction and encouragement helped me to not only write a chapter, but now a book. I am proud to say I am an author and without you, I would have kept delaying and telling myself "next time." Thank you for your vision.

I would like to thank Linnette Tompkins, a very talented artist, for hand painting the vision for my book cover and giving it life. You painted my vision as I described it. Thank you very much.

My desire is to leave a legacy of who I am for my loved ones, which includes every breath I take. To my Angels in Heaven: Gramma, Mommy, my grandfather Dodo, my grandmother Helen, my brother LaShawn and Daddy, I pray that you are looking down on me with a huge smile. You were my strength during my weakest times and now as I celebrate this achievement, it would be disrespectful to not honor you, as you are always with me. To my loved ones on Earth, I'm not alone in this journey because you are always supporting me in my vision, endeavors and attempts, and for that, I love you unconditionally. I want you all to be proud to say, "That's my wife, mother, grandmother, sister, niece, cousin, friend and confidant". I want them to also say, "She endured and overcame the worst of the worst and still stands tall".

Introduction

I, Tracy L. Tate Jones, first shared my story in the compilation book, Broken into Brilliance Volume II, Chapter title From the Frying Pan into the Fire. I told the story of going from one bad relationship into one that was worse, the fear of dying, the shame of rape, and the losses I endured that controlled my life. Five Years in the Fog is the continuation of that story.

I thought I was with the love of my life, until that tragic day in 1995. A few years earlier, we met under unusual circumstances, but his charm and caring nature was refreshing. After being with someone that loved multiple females, to falling for someone that should have been off-limits and chose addiction over love, to being young and dumb, the relationship with Mister was a dream. Mister was very caring to me and my son. Since I had walked away from my son's father and his family to escape addiction, finding a family man was refreshing. I always considered my son's father's house as an addiction trap for me. Everything was too accessible to remain clean and sober. With Mister, we went everywhere together and were a nice little family all the time. All truth came to light after Mister served time in jail for drug possession. It wasn't the fact that he was a bad boy that came to light, it was the fact that he was just like my ex, needing to be loved by multiple females. I just knew he was not that type, or at least that is what I thought.

Introduction

How dare he cheat on me, I thought to myself. I didn't think he was very good looking so I guess I thought I had it in the bag. My ex was a "pretty" bad boy, so I thought a not so pretty bad boy was better. WRONG!! Boy did I know how to pick them bad boys. Once I found out who he really was my feelings for him started to change.

I began trying to keep busy away from Mister, so I enrolled in school for my bachelor's degree. It was a way to escape the truth of who Mister was. Somehow, I decided that men will be men and that cheating was a natural occurrence so it didn't bother me so much. Being raised in a home with my great grandmother, whose husband had passed away the year I was born, I never learned what a man/husband was supposed to be. After all, even the boyfriend I had in junior high and high school cheated on me. I always thought, as long as I got what I wanted, he was attentive to me and "put me first", that's all that mattered. My maternal grandfather, Dodo, was present growing up, but as a provider. There was no "parent" relationship to model my life of love after. It was not so much that Mister was cheating; it was that he started to neglect the household to run the streets with other women. I no longer came first. Believe it or not, I still carry this concept of "put me first" and I can care less about what goes on outside of my household. To me, it has nothing to do with me and is none of my business. Or like the saying goes, out of sight, out of mind.

Introduction

After all I've been through with the men in my life, the less baggage the better.

With that being said, I still loved Mister, but he was changing. I never knew Mister had an addiction prior to our relationship, but once his addiction returned the neglect began to surface. His addition came first, which was a problem for me. I tried to stay by my man, but it was not easy for me to accept being second. After all, I have a controlling nature and second place just won't do. To get away from the addiction, we drove to his family's house in another state to get a handle on our relationship, but Mister tried to bring the addiction with us. Not!! We stayed out of state for about a month with no real progress in our relationship. In our haste to get away, we left our belongings in an unsecured place, so we returned home to find most of our stuff gone and had to start over. This was the second time for me, little did he know, but we found support in his family and mine. All of this was before our move to Oakland.

When we moved to Oakland, I began seeing similar patterns of addiction. I too was an addict, but I was a "functioning addict". What the hell is a functioning addict? This means my addiction was recreational, not demanding or habitual. Since I was still in school, my time for recreation was limited. Mister's addiction was demanding and soon became demanding on me. We went out of state to get a handle on his addiction

Introduction

because of that demand and I literally put my work and school on hold to save my family. Mister didn't have a recreational addiction so it became overbearing by the time we lived in Oakland. The night of the assault, Mister and I had a huge argument about the time I needed to complete my class assignments. I was going to put him on the BART, but needed him for carpool in the morning to get to work and didn't have BART fare for him. Mister left as I completed my assignment. When I was finished, I tucked Son into bed in his room, and I went to lie down. Mister returned and woke me up. We stayed up for a short while and then went to sleep.

About an hour later, the sound of the front door being kicked in woke us up. There were 4 goons that came into our home and they seemed very organized. There was a leader, a couple of ruff necks and a youngster. I will never forget the sounds of that night. I could tell the leader was in his late 20s or early 30s, the ruff necks were early 20s and the youngster was under 20. You can tell by the maturity in their speaking who was who. The leader called all the shots and asked all of the questions. The ruff necks followed orders, but were also eager to do damage and were very disrespectful. The youngster was like a puppy on a leash. The damage I endured was from the objects rammed up me before and after the rape. I was also raped more than once in the 5+ hours of the home invasion. Those were the longest 5 hours I've ever

Introduction

had in my life. I wanted to die just to get it over with. The torture was unbearable, but not knowing what was coming next was even worse. I don't know if it was fear, fatigue or if I fainted, but I have no memory of the last hour or two.

I never stepped foot back in that apartment. I was greatly afraid, but was also embarrassed. While I was in the hospital, I got word that the assault hit the news, but also that the neighborhood was praying for me. That meant they knew where I was. That scared the life out of me so I made Hyland Hospital release me early because I was afraid they would come kill me. After all, they clearly stated they would kill us if we went to the police. Knowing I was in the hospital meant just that, we went to the police and they knew it. While I was in the hospital, the neighborhood helped themselves to our belongings. They took Son's games, our groceries, clothes, shoes, etc., since we did not have a front door anymore. By the time I had someone go get my stuff, there wasn't much left to get. My good friend from work made sure she got everything that was left. We lost almost everything except for our beds and my school books. Go figure.

Many people in the apartment complex only knew me coming and going as I only associated with one person in the 8 unit building. Everyone else just knew my car, my face and that I was only there at night. Every day we arose early in the mornings to commute to San Francisco and didn't return until

Introduction

late evening, after work and picking up my son. On weekends, I had assignments to do or we visited family in SF. I didn't know anything about Oakland, but I did know my cousin didn't live far from us. I just wasn't the socializing type and kept to myself. Mister, on the other hand, was not that type. They clearly knew him so he was there more often then I knew of. Lord knows what he did in our apartment when I was at work or school. This traumatic event went on to haunt me drastically over the next 5 years of my life, as I endured day-by-day in a fog. It took me about 10 years to be able to drive past the exit on the freeway without feeling a huge pit in my stomach. I was gravely scared of that area, even the highway exit.

Year 1_In the Frying Pan; One Tragedy to the Next

It was one thing to endure the traumatic actions of strangers, but it cuts that much deeper when you endure similar tragedies from someone you love(d). Mister was once my forever love, but all of that changed. What happened to the man I fell in love with? Where was the southern charm that won my heart, or had I just been infatuated with someone I thought was different? I remember that Mister didn't have rhythm at all, but we danced as if no one was watching. I often had to turn my back while dancing to not get off rhythm too. How funny. Those were the good old days.

After the traumatic rape, I hid out for a while to sort through the emotions away from Son. When I returned from hiding out at my cousin's house down the highway, I got an apartment for me, Son and Mister. At that time, I hadn't heard the rumors about him being the cause of the home invasion because I had been hiding out. I was still grateful to not have endured that traumatic event alone. I wanted our relationship to work again, like it had been in the beginning. Mister was so compassionate, gentle and thoughtful. He put our family first. He was supportive of my education and work and made sure Son was looked after. After the traumatic event it didn't take long for word to get back to me once I was no longer in hiding.

My cousin, whose house we ran to after the home invasion in Oakland, had been asking around about what happened. She never let it be known that she was my family, so people openly talked about it with her. She found out a lot of scoop about what was going on while I would be at work. Mister would return to Oakland after dropping me off at work and rent the car out to fuel his addiction. Remember, he was a bad boy so he didn't work, only hustled. He was also running people around here and there for money. Unknown to me, my car was a rental car in the neighborhood prior to that traumatic day. She learned that he would often be with the female from downstairs, the one whose apartment was invaded too. That is why those intruders knew him and thought I was the female he had been with.

Hearing this new information was enough to turn my feelings completely 180 degrees. I had been grateful to not have endured that trauma alone, but it quickly turned into "It would have never happened it if wasn't for him". I was no longer grateful; I was disgusted and pissed that he would allow that to happen to me and be the cause of it. He never said anything about what happened when we reunited, so it was like he lied to me about being the reason it happened. HE NEVER APOLOGIZED FOR IT either. How could he think I would forgive him for this? The more information I received, the more hatred I felt for Mister. Eventually I told him I wanted out.

Year 1_In the Frying Pan; One Tragedy to the Next

He wanted our relationship to work, but for me I was done. Between being cheated on, dealing with addiction, to physical fights and then a home invasion caused by him, I WAS DONE.

At first, it seemed amicable that we were separating and both of us were fine with it; however, Mister was trying to earn forgiveness. He started doing things he hadn't done in a while, like buying flowers, bringing me lunch at work, etc., although it didn't impress me. I also allowed him to still see my son since he was the only father my son had seen and known since he was about 2 years old. That was his daddy. I thought that was best for my son, especially since he had witnessed the traumatic event too. I wanted a father figure in his life, since his dad was not around him. BIG MISTAKE. Mister used my son as a pawn to pop up or come over all the time. My son once said, "Daddy why do you always watch my mama sleeping?" I hadn't thought too much of it at the time, but after the next events unfolded, it was alarming. When Mister would come see Son, I left them to play and minded my business. Mister was just there to spy and to try to get his foot back in the door.

A couple of months after I got my new apartment in San Francisco and moved Mister out, my son reunited with his dad's side of the family. It was easy to connect now that we lived so close to them. He would go spend time with his other siblings and I would go wash clothes. One day I returned home to find my bedroom window broken. We lived in the downstairs unit of a duplex. Mister was sitting outside on the stairs waiting for me to get home. He had shattered the bedroom window from pounding on it, thinking I was at home and wouldn't answer the door. Hell if I had been home asleep, as he thought, all of the glass from the broken window would have landed in my head. When I entered my room, the glass was on my pillow and on the nightstand on my side of the bed. He kept apologizing and got the window fixed quickly. It didn't scare me at the time, but again, as events unfolded and thinking back on it after the fact, these were more signs of Mister coming unhinged.

The following week, Mister came to visit Son and didn't want to leave. I kept asking him to leave and said I would call the police if he didn't. He was angry because he wanted to have sex and I didn't. He kept the excuse going that he was waiting for Son to fall to sleep. I couldn't go to sleep until he was gone so I kept trying to put him out. The more I pushed, the angrier he got. After about an hour of arguing for him to leave, he angrily got up to leave, but argued the whole way out the door. I tried to slam the door behind him because by this time I was pissed that he was keeping us up so late and wouldn't leave. As he walked out the door, I went to slam the door and he stopped it with his feet and kicked it. I yelled at him for

Year 1_In the Frying Pan; One Tragedy to the Next

doing that and he kicked it again. By this time he was completely in a rage and kept closing the door to kick it back open. He kicked it so hard that the door split in two, directly down the middle. There was no way to fix it and it was way after mid-night by this time. The entire time he was kicking the door I was on the phone with 911 telling them what he was doing as he closed and kicked the door over and over. By the time police arrived, he had gone. All they could do was take a report, as it was a domestic issue. Since he had been a resident for over 30 days, there was nothing they could do.

I called an old friend to see if he could come fix the door for me. He came with one of his friends, who turned out to be my Knight. They put the closet door from the bedroom on the front door to get the cold off of us and secure the home. They even stayed with us to make sure we were ok. I hadn't seen Old Friend in a long time, but knew I could always call him if I needed him. He was often in jail for one thing or another so we didn't see each other much. When he was out, he always made sure I knew he was home. I was so thankful for them coming in the middle of the night and securing us. During the next week, somehow, Old Friend and Mister connected. I can't even tell you how they were introduced, but it was not long that Mister got Old Friend out the picture. That same week, he and Mister went to Daly City to a Liquor Barn to steal liquor. As Old Friend was coming out the store with the stolen goods,

Year 1_In the Frying Pan; One Tragedy to the Next

Mister was supposed to drive up and pick him up at the door. That didn't happen. Instead, Mister drove off and left Old Friend to get caught. Just as Mister drove off, police were pulling up. It seemed as though Mister had set up Old Friend. Even if he didn't, he got what he wanted, and that was Old Friend out the way. He knew Old Friend was my ex that still had feelings for me and he surely didn't want Old Friend around.

The week after that, Mister came to visit with Son after apologizing over and over for his actions. This was the only dad my son really knew so I didn't want to keep Mister from him. I just didn't want to be in a relationship with him anymore. As it was getting later and later, I asked him to leave so we could get ready for school and work the next day. He told me he would not leave unless I had sex with him. He knew I did not want anything to do with him and I kept declining. Over and over I asked him to leave and he would not. He would say "I'll leave if you have sex with me". I told him that if he had sex with me it would be him raping me all over again. This was literally 5 months after the home invasion in Oakland, if that. He kept grabbing my clothes and pulling them off. I told him over and over that he would be raping me if he had sex with me because I didn't want it. He would not stop and kept trying to have sex. As he lay on top of me, stroking, I repeated over and over, "You are raping me, you are raping me, YOU ARE RAPING ME" and cried. When he was finished, he got up and

Year 1_In the Frying Pan; One Tragedy to the Next

started putting his clothes on. I just lay there crying, waiting for him to leave. Just as he was putting his pants on, I got a call from Knight, checking on us since he knew Old Friend had gone back to jail. He could tell in my voice that something was wrong. I kept lying, saying I was ok, but he said he was coming over to see for himself. Mister heard the one-sided conversation. He did leave, but soon returned to "tuck" Son into bed, so he said.

Mister had returned and was in my son's room when Knight and his friend came to check on us. Everything was fine until Knight was leaving and asked if I wanted Mister to leave with them. I told him yes, so Knight went in Son's room to ask Mister to leave with him and his friend. Not a second went by before I heard screaming from Son's room, "He's stabbing me, he's stabbing me". Oh my God, Mister completely lost his mind. He was stabbing Knight over and over and in front of Son. NOT AGAIN, the trauma. Mister was in a complete rage, swinging the knife at Knight and his friend, barely missing me. I was screaming, jumping around trying to get to Son and trying to call 911. Their fighting had moved to the living room and the phone got tangled up in the melee. I ran out the front door to my neighbor's, yelling to call 911. By this time the fighting and stabbing had moved outside. Mister was chasing me and Knight's friend around the parked cars as Knight lay on the floor, helpless. He had been stabbed several times.

Mister kept saying, "I'm dying", but continued to chase us with the knife. Mister had also been stabbed in the fighting. I was scared shitless. Several police cars pulled up and I ran into the house to Son. As soon as I entered the door, I saw there was blood everywhere and Knight was on the floor, bleeding to death. I thought for sure Mister had killed him. Pieces of his liver were on the wall, blood splatter and prints went from the back of the house where Son's room was, all the way through the hall to the living room. It was a blood bath. What just happened?? All I wanted was for him to leave. It was horrible, and all in front of my son, yet again. This was way too much for a 7 year old to see and hear, again. My little man stayed strong and tried to comfort me as I cried and screamed about what had just happened. I called his dad's sister to watch him while I went to the police station to give my side of the story. I could not stop crying for hours, even at the police station when I was giving my statement. They had a record of the domestic incident the weeks prior when he kicked in the door, but this was far beyond any of our imaginations. The RAGE he had was like he had taken a narcotic or something. His eyes were wide open, the size of eggs, and very dark. The police instructed me to get a restraining order because Mister had not died and would probably come back. It was also good to learn that Knight would survive too. What a relief. All he was trying to do was to make sure me and Son were ok, and almost got killed. JUST CRAZY.

Year 1_In the Frying Pan; One Tragedy to the Next

After all we had already been through with the home invasion and now the stabbing, my mind was all over the place. All I could do was think that my life had almost been taken and that Mister was following through on his threat that if he couldn't have me, no one could. He'd said it a couple times before, but I wasn't afraid of him until this event. I thought he was just talking, NOT!! Honestly, I hadn't even thought about Son being traumatized too. He should have gotten therapy right then and there, but during that time of my life, I didn't believe in therapy. The old saying, "What goes on in this house, stays in this house" was prevalent in my logic. I didn't think about how all of this would affect him, even in the long run. I did get him help at school with smaller classes through Special Ed, but even with that, I don't think it helped him much. He had a lot of anger, which was understandable, but it was not okay to act up at school. I am a stickler for education. Not only did he witness these traumatizing events, he also witnessed how it affected his mommy.

While the investigation was happening, I could not go home and did not want to be there anyway. I didn't return for weeks. I stayed with Son at his grandmother's house. Little did I know, the detectives never locked my door so the neighborhood, once again, helped themselves to our belongings. We had just replenished everything that had been taken in Oakland, so this was another blow. My coworkers had replaced my son's games, our TV and even replaced our groceries the first time, but this was a second time, in less than five months, so we were on our own. They took the game console, games, TVs, groceries, clothes, shoes and CDs. NOT AGAIN. This was another violation, almost as bad as the home invasion. It's devastating to have things taken from you without you giving them, whether it is possessions or your body, especially since we had just replaced them. Yet another traumatizing event, but even after this I went back to work as if nothing happened. Most people would have lost their minds. Well I did eventually, but initially I buried my mental emotions in my work.

Year 2_In the Fire; What Knight?

Weeks after the stabbing happened, I went to check on Knight. He truly saved my life that day. I was ever so grateful for him being there and was very sorry for what had happened to him. The friend that was with him didn't get hurt, or maybe not that bad, but I don't know because I never saw him again. All I could do was say, "Thank you" and "I'm sorry" to Knight over and over. That was the first day I met his mom. She was a very loving woman; that I will never forget. I apologized to her also for what had happened to her son. I went back upstairs to check on Knight only to have his girlfriend at the time jump on me because her man got injured. The entire incident with Mister truly caught me off-guard, who knew Mister was capable of such things. I would have never gotten Old Friend or Knight involved in my domestic issues. I just wanted out. I continued to check on Knight over the next couple of months as he healed. In that time, I fell for him and he for me. I saw him as heroic, gentle and loving, especially to Son. He would get down on the floor and wrestle with Son and play with him, something I never saw Mister do, so it was enticing. He also knew what Son had witnessed and it was a relief to see him try to keep Son's mind off of the traumatic event.

After several months of interacting, Knight moved in with us. I never thought about the traumatic memories he would have being back in a place that almost got him killed. I don't know if this is what changed him or not, but it wasn't long that I saw who Knight truly was. Knight also had an addiction problem and it resurfaced. Of course I knew he was an addict because we got high together after the time the door was kicked in, but we both vowed to end the addiction after the stabbing event. We figured we were given a second opportunity at life instead of losing our lives that night. One day Knight left for work and didn't return for a few days. I called the police to file a missing person's report; how naïve of me to do. It's funny now, but I was oh so serious when I reported him missing. He returned a few days later, and even then I never suspected anything of it. That was the start of the worst couple of years of my life. Over the next two years, every day became worse and worse.

Knight soon lost his job and would be gone for days at a time. By this time, I knew his addition had returned in full force, but didn't know what to do. After all, this man saved my life. I continued to work and live as normal until it all changed for me. I was reintroduced to my addiction myself, but in a new way. Knight was either home with me while getting high or gone for days. I was always afraid of how smoking the pipe changed people for the worse, but after all, I had been a functioning addict for so long that I thought it would be the same. Boy was I wrong. All I knew was this new way kept Knight at home instead of away for days at a time. I was a

Year 2_In the Fire; What Knight?

functioning addict as usual, until one day I was not. I began missing work, not paying bills, running the streets, and had truly become someone I didn't know. Soon after beginning getting high again, the physical abuse started. This made me miss more days from work because I was too embarrassed to show the bruises. My coworkers knew something was not right because I was physically changing, but also mentally changing. I was becoming depressed because one thing that Knight started saying was "If I can't have you, no one can." Well after the traumatic event with Mister, I took him for his word. I was afraid to leave him, although I saw I was becoming someone I didn't know or like.

I began lying and scheming to get money for my addiction. I was raised to never lie, cheat or steal and I began doing them all. Who is this person? This is not the lady I was raised to be, or was it? Growing up I was always told, "You gone be just like your mother." My mother was a drug addict and I was always ashamed of her as a kid. I even told people that my mother was deceased so other kids wouldn't ask me where she was or why I was not living with her. Everyone knew I lived with my great grandmother, so they surely asked. Well the questions stopped when I started that rumor. Well the truth came out at my 8th grade graduation as my mother came into the Catholic church, beautiful and proud. It was then that I saw past her addiction, but still didn't want to be like her. Well with

Knight, that was exactly what I was being: an addict, just like my mother.

One day I had rented a car for a couple of days. When it was time to return it, Knight was nowhere to be found. He was gone with it for days and days after it was due back at Budget. When he returned, I begged him to return it, but he wouldn't, and like always, beat me up and left again. I think he may have been lending the rental car out to get money for himself. I don't know but I know he wouldn't let me return the car. Budget called me after 3 weeks and I told them that the person I rented it for wouldn't return it and to report it stolen. I told them there was nothing I could do. I was so hoping that Knight would get caught in it and would go to jail; that would get him out of my life. Little did I know that when the police caught up with the car, because there was a minor in the car that we knew, I had to turn myself into the police station. The officer that responded to the door being kicked in by Mister had also responded to the night Mister stabbed Knight and when I called to report Knight missing, Laugh Out Loud, he called to tell me to turn myself in so he wouldn't have to come handcuff me in front of Son. He knew what Son had witnessed and wanted to spare him some more drama with his mama. So I turned myself in the next morning after Son went to school. I thought I would be released quickly, but I was at the station for about 8 hours. I had to call my upstairs neighbor to pick

Year 2_In the Fire; What Knight?

me up from the police station. When I got home, Knight was there partying with his friend and girlfriend, not even thinking about me and the traumatic experience I had at the police station. I was a good girl so I had never been arrested before, let alone put in a holding cell, taken upstairs to shower and be put in a cell with other women at 850 Bryant St in SF. How humiliating.

After several months of being in my addiction and enduring abuse, Knight moved his other woman into the apartment with us. What the hell???!!! I was so afraid of him by this time, I didn't know what to do but accept it. I made sure I was the dominant one between us, but she learned how to turn it around on me. She would tell Knight lies to get me in trouble and he would beat me for it. By this time, he would beat me for anything. I hated her for that, so every chance I got, I tried to make her suffer. Son was present for all of this madness, although I thought he didn't know what was going on. It wasn't until he was almost grown that I learned he witnessed the abuse and the other mess that went on inside our home, like being stalked in the bathroom and followed around. One day while taking a shower, as I was getting out to dry off, I hadn't even noticed Knight was staring through the bathroom window at me until he made a noise and I looked up and saw him looking at me. I almost jumped out my skin. I never knew that he would often watch me through the bathroom and kitchen window. It scared the daylights out of me because he said I would never be able to leave him and that he was always watching me. Well that was proof.

Not long after learning of him watching and following me, I was talking to his mother on the phone. By this time I had already lost my job due to absences and the havoc going on in my life from the home invasion assault, Mister 's traumatizing acts, to the many absences resulting from abuse and addiction, my employer at the time had enough. I told his mother how Knight always threatened to kill me. I used to tell him, "If you kill me, take my son too". I was all my son had since his dad and his side of the family where not very present; at least he didn't know them well and my family members were busy trying to raise their own children. His mother told me that he was just talking out the side of his neck. Even she didn't know I was being physically abused, at least I think she didn't know. I was so embarrassed about whom I had become, I stayed away from everyone. Well on another day when talking to her, I was at my wits end and felt like giving up. I felt like I had lost everything, especially myself. I told his mother, "All I can do is beat him to the punch." She asked me what I was talking about. I told her there would be a double funeral. "I have to kill him before he kills me". She begged me not to say that. Knight's other woman overheard the conversation and of course told him. She thought I was talking about her and him,

Year 2_In the Fire; What Knight?

but I was actually talking about me and him. Well she didn't stay in my house long after that. Clearly I scared her off, but it also made Knight stay gone longer. It was a good thing, but he made sure I knew he was always watching, which kept me scared. He always returned when my unemployment check was coming, and then would take all of my money and stay gone.

Little did I know depression had overpowered my mental state of mind. One day after Knight had abused me, taken the money I had left after paying bills, and then left the apartment, I went into a hysterical rage. I knocked over furniture, I pulled all of the drawers out the dressers, all the kitchen cabinets were opened, and stuff thrown all over the floor. I needed a cigarette and couldn't find one. I grabbed our pit bull, Sugga, and headed to the store. It was the middle of the night so no stores were open. Me and that dog walked ten blocks each direction before getting to a store where I could buy a single cigarette. We returned home to me walking in on all of that mess. My son and his half-brother were hiding in his bed under the covers. I hadn't known it was me that caused the damage and mess. I walked in and asked "Son who been in the house and tore it up"? To my surprise, he answered, "It was you, Mama". Apparently the fresh air snapped me out of it, but I hadn't even known what had already occurred. I had a nervous breakdown in front of my children!!! I always thought depression and nervous breakdowns were excuses until I had one. Lord help me.

About a month after the revelation that I would kill him before he killed me, we had to move. I couldn't pay for the apartment anymore since I wasn't working and the little money I did get, Knight would take it. I had found a job for a short while, but didn't keep it due to absences and I didn't get past the probationary period. The sheriff had to remove us because I had nowhere to go. The day the sheriff came to evict us, Knight had been gone all morning instead of at home helping me pack the truck. I was livid. I had to move with nowhere to go and didn't have help to get it done. We got locked out with all of our stuff in the apartment. It was that day that I saw how Knight had been able to access the side of the house to watch me in the bathroom and removed the windows to get into the house. We quickly loaded the truck and took our things to a storage unit. I had received a motel voucher from the county for 30 days. That was nowhere I wanted Son to be so I sent him to stay with his dad's family. By this time, the FOG had begun.

Year 3 _ Homelessness; Everything Lost

Although I could have received support from my family, I felt all alone and embarrassed by what had happened in my life. I'd prided myself on my education and working, so getting caught up in all of this madness was too much to reveal to my family. I kept them out of my business and relied on support from people that I really didn't know, and they didn't know me. With them there wasn't really any embarrassment or shame because they didn't know my upbringing or my accomplishments; however, my family did. Growing up, everyone was talked about when things weren't going right in their lives, so I didn't want the criticism or to hear the infamous saying, "You're going to be just like your mother". I had been through enough already and didn't allow my family to know the facts of what I'd been through. They knew some things like the rape and the incident with Mister, but many of them didn't know about my eviction or the abuse from Knight. They knew I was on drugs, but probably didn't know to what extent initially because I'd always been a functioning addict, so there was nothing really to talk about. I handled my business as I was supposed to. They only knew what I wanted them to know.

Staying at the motel brought a lot of anger out of me and I was completely out of my mind. I can recall an incident when

Year 3 _ Homelessness; Everything Lost

Knight was in another room at the motel and had stolen my money or did something to me and I lost it. He was in the room and they would not answer the door, but I could hear them in there. What I can recall is me breaking the window to their room to get in. I'm not a violent person and was never aggressive, but something changed in me after my nervous breakdown. It was just all too much; one thing after another and nothing was familiar to me. I went from being a hardworking person, a good student, a mother, a provider, and independent to someone I didn't recognize and didn't want to be. It was all gone. I began depending on the system to get help; I didn't have Son with me and was nowhere near independent anymore. After the 30 day voucher was up, Knight and I moved in with his mom. I am forever grateful for her hospitality. She got to see firsthand how her son was mistreating me. I know she was ashamed, as I found out many years later, after she passed and I became sober that she left me two insurance policies for $1,000 each. I found them in the unclaimed funds left at the state. Even though they didn't say who the policy holder was, I know it was her by the address and the old name I had while I lived with her. I think about her often. She is forever in my heart. I can remember her saying "You changed. You are letting him drag you down".

While we were staying with his mom, he continued to abuse me mentally and physically. There were times that he was

Year 3 _ Homelessness; Everything Lost

loving and gentle, but when I finally started receiving GA and every time I got money, he would find a reason to beat me up and take my money, like he always had. This went on for months. I would barely go around my family or Son because I was always bruised up. Luckily for me my skin heals quickly so it wasn't long before I could hide the bruises on the outside. The bruises on the inside were another story. He would threaten me that if I left while he was gone, he would find me and kill me. Although I thought about killing him before he could me, it just wasn't in my nature. It was a wishful dream to escape the nightmare. Being in the addiction also helped escape the nightmare, but accessing drugs and alcohol was not easy. It always seemed that no sooner did I find alcohol or drugs; he would pop up and take them or use them up. He had to be watching me or had other people watching me so he knew my every move. Imagine living life in fear day in and day out. I just didn't care to live anymore. It was just too much to handle.

One of the biggest mistakes I ever made in my life was giving up. I didn't consider the impact it would have on Son, especially after all he had witnessed the prior year. I just wanted out of the nightmare. It was my faith that kept me from committing suicide, although I considered it more than once. Giving up meant that Son was not being cared for by me. I gave birth to him at the age of 19, turning 20, and he was all I

Year 3 _ Homelessness; Everything Lost

had to live for. Although I was ashamed, afraid and tired, my love for my son kept me pushing. He would come visit me at Knight's mom's house or I would go see him at his grandmother's house. Those were the only times I had peace, mentally and physically. Often times, my addition overpowered my wants. I never wanted my son to see me high so I would leave him or cut our time together short. Addiction brings out the devil in you.

Up until that day that I ran down the dirt trail, I was abused almost daily. I was finally tired of the abuse and living in fear. After one of the beatings for no reason, I ran downstairs to his mom, gave her a kiss on the cheek and a strong hug and said, "Mama, I can't do this anymore. Thank you for everything, but you will never see me again". With tears in her eyes she said, "I know". I peeked out the back door to make sure I didn't see Knight anywhere and ran as fast as I could. I didn't take anything with me, just the clothes I had on my back. I ran and ran to the main street outside of the projects and saw the #29 bus coming. I jumped on the bus, ducked down and begged the driver to let me ride for free. I was running so fast, I actually ran past the bus stop and just flagged him down. Several stops later, I got off the bus and ran to my cousin's house who lived nearby. I just cried and cried and said I needed to get out of there. They had a white van, and she had her son take me to snatch up Son and hightail it out of there. I don't even recall if I

Year 3 _ Homelessness; Everything Lost

told his grandmother I was taking him. I just knew I had to get me and Son out of there.

We went to Oakland and stayed with my aunt for a couple of months. That was the most peace I had in a couple of years. Although I was still not independent, I was at peace, even from my addiction. After several months, it was time to get Son back to his grandmother so he could go to school. I was homeless, but he wasn't. I would spend the night with him sometimes, but for the most part, I started running the streets again. I gained the strength to not be in fear anymore, as I remember seeing Knight again and recalled an incident when I lived with him and his mom when a neighborhood dude was looking to fight him. Knight kept running from him so I got to see firsthand what a coward he was. He would fight women, but not men. It also helped that my son's grandmother lived across the street from the neighborhood OG that liked me. I met him before I got evicted and would often get free stuff from him. He became my OG. Being with OG, I felt safe and secure. He made sure I was not on the streets. He even gave me a job as his personal assistant. I did all of his paperwork for his construction jobs and he kept me with food, drinks, and drugs. I was safe, but I was far from independent or sober.

Year 4_ Lost in Addiction

Before I connected with my OG, I was lost in mental, physical, and drug abuse. I'm sure depression was a factor too, but I always thought depression was an excuse. It was easier to just stay numb to reality so that's what I did. This was the first time in my life that I was lost beyond my imagination. I had hit my rock bottom. I had never lost so much in my life, and the shame I had from being raped, losing my job, losing my home and being physically abused was far too much to think about. So while I was getting high, all of those things were farthest from my thoughts. I focused on how I would get my next piece of dope and bottle of gin. That was a daily struggle in itself, but it kept me occupied. I would stay up for many hours and sometimes days searching for drugs and getting high. There was always someone around with dope to share, but no one would support your habit. I always felt like people I got high with would "get me started" just to manipulate me into getting or wanting more. Now that I know how addiction works, it was actually them looking out for themselves, because once it was gone, it wasn't easy getting more. I used to ask Son for money and pay him back double what he gave me. Although I didn't like being around him while I was high, I know he knew I did drugs. The personality was too present around him. He was the only person that I could count on that wouldn't play games with me. I always explained to him that I was sick, but it's nothing he should have had to witness at his age. Unfortunately, during that time, the crack epidemic was in full force and there were a lot of parents caught up in addiction just like me.

As time went by, I got closer and closer to OG. He made sure I was taken care of, but of course that came with a price. At that time, he was the best thing that happened to me. I was no longer walking the streets to stay awake when I had nowhere to live. I stayed at his house often, and it was convenient being across the street from Son's grandmother so I was able to see him all the time. I went to work with OG every day to do the painting for his construction company. It allowed me to earn my keep so to speak. I made money to buy the things I wanted, mostly drink and drugs, but it also allowed me to be away from drinking and drugs for a good portion of the day. He also helped me get a place to stay in public housing. I didn't have furniture at first because I had lost the storage unit we had when I was evicted due to non-payment, but I had somewhere to lay my head. It was far away from him and Son so I wasn't there much. I even had Son come live with me there, but still stayed away from him when I was chasing dope. My son was only about 9 years old and had to get up by himself, get ready for school and catch the school bus, all without supervision. I wasn't there to see him off to school, to make sure he had food to eat, to help him with his homework or even to make sure he had clean clothes to put on. I was a hot mess, lost in addiction. I relied on my neighbors to make sure he was safe, but didn't think about me neglecting his needs. I would be away for the whole week before coming back. I would call him, but I wouldn't go home to care for him. The thing is, I raised him to care for himself at an early age. Before all of the madness we endured, I was a workaholic and worked at home a lot, so I taught him how to cook food, wash his clothes, and get himself ready for school. He would often make my dinner while I worked. He was only about 5 then, so even when I was gone chasing dope, he knew he had better get up and get ready for the school bus or he would be in trouble. I wasn't caring for him, but if he didn't take care of himself, he would get in big trouble. I was a strict mother, even in addiction.

One day I was near his grandmother's house and he came to see me where I was washing clothes for OG. He rode a bike up to see me. I didn't know the bike didn't have breaks, but he was a daredevil on wheels. After leaving me on his way back to his grandmother's house, he was hit by a car and they left him on the side of the street. I got the call and nearly jumped out of my skin. When I got to the accident site, I cried uncontrollably. I was there with him the first few hours, but I left to feed my addiction. After a while, I returned and went straight to sleep. By this point in life, I was becoming more of an alcoholic. It was cheaper to get a $2 bottle of gin or vodka then it was to get drugs, so I found myself drinking more. Plus I was tired of the crack game, as I called it. Son stayed in the hospital for several weeks before he was released. I would go up to see him almost every night, but when I did, I was always sleeping and reeked of alcohol. The nurses reported my condition to CPS. They officially placed my son with his grandmother to be cared for when he got released. He had to get pins put in his leg to keep it intact. He was on a walker and crutches for a long while and had to go through physical therapy to learn to walk on that leg again. Even to this day, when the weather changes, he gets pain in his leg. Through it all, he still smiles.

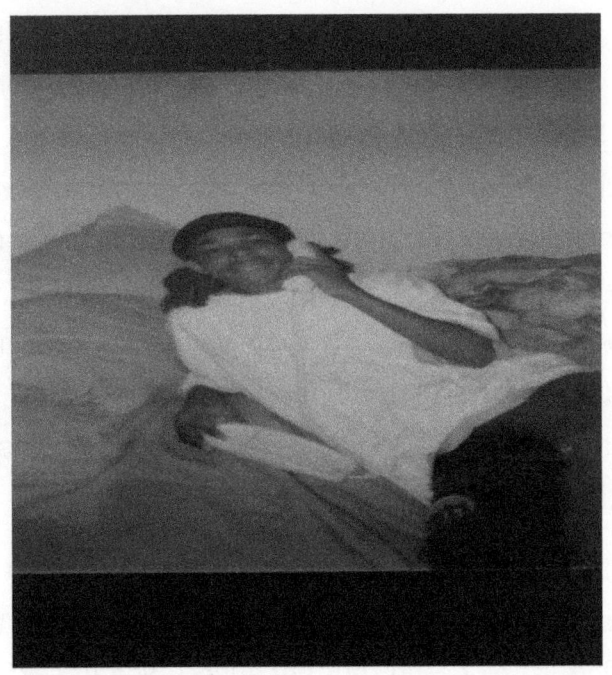

One day I went to visit Son at his grandmother's house and he said something disrespectful, which I did not tolerate even on drugs, so I chastised him. His grandmother didn't like it and kicked me out. I never thought she would keep my son from me, but she did and that hurt me to the core. I recalled Knight always telling me that Son's grandmother would try to take Son from me but thought he was lying. When she kicked me out and wouldn't let me see him again, my depression and addiction got worse before it got better. How could she keep me from the only thing I had left in life? She knew I had been leaving him home alone when he stayed with me because she would see me at all times of the morning and night, but he was nowhere around. When CPS placed him with his grandmother, I didn't mind him being cared for by her because

I knew I was not caring for him correctly. But I also never expected her to prevent me from seeing and loving him, although I loved the fact that he was getting close to his dad and his side of the family. For me, his grandmother's house was a crack haven because of where it was located. It was very easy to get drugs, so it kept me with drugs, but I was also scared to be around there. This is why I had kept him away from his family for so long when I was with Mister. It wasn't good for me, but at this point in my addiction, it was perfect, with easy access to drugs and alcohol.

Weeks later, I thought about putting myself in a drug program for the first time. It was easier said than done. I had to be put on a waiting list to get in, but because I was in CPS and my cousin had connections in the program, they helped me get on the list quickly. By that time I had compromised every moral and value I was raised with and was so lost wallowing in guilt, shame, and embarrassment, and had no will to live. When Son was taken from me, at first I was like good for him; but when the reality set in that I no longer controlled when I could see him, when I could hug him, kiss him or even speak to him, everything was dark for me. This time my will to live was not because of fear or physical abuse, but because of my abuse of drugs and alcohol, an addiction that I couldn't beat on my own. I also didn't have a secured date to enter into the program I was waiting to get into. I couldn't even help myself, let alone help my son. This was an even darker time in my life without Son.

Year 5_ Failed Recovery

When I finally got into the program, it was something new that I wasn't prepared for. I assumed it would be a breeze to do, but boy was I wrong. I was not used to sharing my personal things, thoughts, stories of addiction and surely was not used to sharing a room with 49 other women or sleeping on a bunk bed. There was no privacy, a lot of rules and daily chores. I wasn't used to that either. I was there about a month before I could do an outing, which had to be with a buddy. Two addicts on the loose after 60 days of treatment, was not a good idea. Hell only two weeks into the program, I planned my outing to get high. My buddy knew that and planned the same. We went to my apartment in public housing and met up with OG and her dude who brought the drugs. The first time using again didn't seem that bad, but my buddy was addicted to pills and brought some back with her. That was a wrong move. At meetings, I would see her spacing out because she took the prescription drugs. I was so nervous that she was going to get us caught. Eventually she did get busted and had to get on what's called a "contract", but she failed that, which caused her to leave the program. I had a lot of guilt around that because I felt that I took her out.

On my second outing, I was able to go alone. I was scheduled to spend time with Son, but again I scheduled to get high. Well

that's exactly what I did instead of spending time with Son. When I went back to the program, I didn't even want to go in. I was so ashamed of not spending time with my son and using that time to get high instead. I saw the disappointment in his eyes when I left him, but he still gave me the biggest hug. One thing about Son, he didn't seem to judge me or at least didn't show it. He only loves all of me, even when I do the wrong things. After the rape and other ordeals he'd witnessed, I think he saw himself as my protector, by all means necessary. Since I had gotten high more than once, the guilt of neglecting spending time on my outing with Son and the guilt of my buddy on the first outing leaving the program finally got to me. The next day I left the program without notice and went back to what my life was about, getting high and drunk.
SHAMEFUL.

Getting high again after leaving the program was like nothing had changed. I thought for sure it would be like starting over. NOT!! I picked right back up where I left off and it only got worse from there. I started entertaining men to get high. No I was not a prostitute, but would befriend any man that was getting high too, to get a free high. Because of my personality, I didn't have to sleep with them to get what I wanted. I had what's called "a gift of gab", and rather a peaceful high. A lot people that smoked would get paranoid and get others around them paranoid in the process. I was not that kind of doper. I liked to chill and keep to myself. People would pay to just get high around me in peace. They never had to worry about their safety or me stealing from them. I asked for what I wanted and usually got what I wanted, even from OG. He kept me in addiction just giving me what I wanted. This time my addition was a little bit different. Since I had a failed recovery, I knew what to expect in the program when I was ready. I learned what I would have to do to get into recovery and what I would have to face. I wasn't ready to do that so I left. I tried to do recovery for Son, but that's not how recovery works. You have to recover for yourself, no one else.

In the meantime, I continued to get high. Although OG gave me everything I asked for, I had a sense of a lack of control. He wasn't controlling, but he controlled everything. He had the power and ability to say no and often times he did. I didn't like that, but endured it. I have a strong sense of loyalty and appreciation for people that often makes me stay in situations that are not always in my best interest or are a good situation for me. Even with Knight, I was appreciative for him coming to my rescue when the door was kicked in and when Mister stabbed him up, but everyone and everything don't deserve loyalty, especially when it is at a cost of oneself. I lost everything due to fear, but it started as loyalty. My OG kept me grounded, but he also kept me addicted. Beating an addiction is hard to do when it's easy to access. It's even harder when it's something you like to do. I've been indulging in drugs and alcohol since a young age, but remember, I considered myself a functioning addict. I lost the functioning part of my addiction during my trials and tribulations, but had gotten back to it when I was working for OG every day. I've worked since I was sixteen years old so it was something familiar to me and made me feel a little like my old self. Is there such a thing? If nothing else, it definitely gave me something to do other than get high all day and I was also able to see Son again.

My son had moved in with his step-mom for a short period. Honestly, I don't know why he wasn't staying with his grandmother anymore, but he was being cared for and was spending time with his siblings so I loved that. His step-mom never denied me access to spend time with Son either. I would go spend the night with them. They even moved into the apartment I had in public housing for a little while. Soon after that I put myself back on the list to re-enter the drug program. At this point, I was tired of being tired. Getting high wasn't an enjoyment for me anymore. The dope was changing and I didn't like how it made me feel so I drank more than anything. When I relisted, I was tired of that life altogether. Son was growing up and I was missing it all. Something had to change. I had to change. This time I was doing it because I wanted to, not because I had to for Son. He was being taken good care of so I was able to just focus on me and what I was escaping from. Starting my recovery journey for me was the best decision I made for myself. I was back to wanting to live and not being a victim anymore. My entire mindset and attitude about everything was changing. I couldn't wait to get back to the program. I spent many days and nights talking to and praying to my angels: my great grandmother, my mother, my grandfather and my maternal grandmother.

While waiting to get back into the program, I had met a guy. There was something about him and I couldn't understand the effect he had on me. He was from the neighborhood where I was living in public housing. Anytime he came around to visit a roommate I had at the time, I would stop drinking, smoking and/or drugging and put it all away until he left. I didn't know why and still don't, but I knew he was heaven sent. I called him My Angel and even sang Anita Baker's song, "You're my Angel" to him. I fell for him hard. He too was a bad boy. What is it with me and these bad boys? It didn't even matter as I guess it was the way he looked at me and saw me. He didn't see my addiction; he saw me. He knew I was an addict, but still cared and chose me to be with. He made wanting to be in recovery easy. I knew when I put my drink and cigarettes away that he was different. He didn't smoke, drink or do drugs ever, but the neighborhood was full of it. I guess that attracted me to him also. He didn't give into temptation or the environment around him. I didn't understand, but drinking and drugs were not a priority when he was around. After being with OG for so long, I saw that My Angel wouldn't cater to my addiction like OG did, which was just what I needed and wanted in my life. Now, seventeen years later, he is still my rock.

Successful Recovery

When I was finally allowed to return to the program, it was one of the happiest days of my life. I was truly tired of being tired. The first day, they made me sit in a chair at the front door. That was their psychological way of saying "There's the front door, leave if you want". Well I stayed that day. Even the next day they had me sitting at the front door again. I stayed again. I was then placed on "contract", which was a punishment for leaving. They called it AWOL. I had to do whatever I was told without talking back. I had to be up at 8am and work continuously until 9pm. I had to clean and mop the metal stairs outside in the rain; I even got sick, but kept going. I also had to clean and mop the kitchen and hallways, had to sit in the corner for hours and was only allowed to get up to use the bathroom, and I was put in the hot seat to be grilled for why I left in the first place. I was on contract for two months, although others had gotten off contract within weeks. I didn't even care. I was so grateful to be allowed back. This would be a tough and long journey but I was ready. During the grilling, I was asked about the buddy pass I had and whether I had gotten high that day. I admitted it. They also blamed me for my buddy leaving the program, but I defended myself against that. I admitted that I had felt guilt initially, but honestly she was a grown woman like me and needed to take responsibility for her own actions as I was doing. I sat there and was grilled about my actions, but also had to be voted back into the house. Some of the people that had stuck and stayed were still there and voted me back in. They gave me a lot of support and praised me for enduring all of the things I had while on contract, especially mopping the stairs in the rain. Now the hard work began!

One of the classes I had in the program was called Grief and Loss. That was a life changer for me. I didn't realize how much hurt and pain I had suppressed for so long. After losing my great-grandmother that raised me at 14, then losing my mother at 19 right before I gave birth to Son, my daddy the following year, my grandfather at 24 and my grandmother at 29, I had a lot of suppressed anger, confusion, and hurt bottled up in layers. After losing all of these loved ones I "worked" the pain off and eventually stayed numb by getting high. I used work to forget about the losses of loved ones and the pain of them not being in my life anymore. I knew if any of them were still alive, my life would have been different. Death is a part of life, but it's something you never get over. It's worse when you don't get the help you need or to talk through the pain. In this class I had to role play about losing my mother. See, my mother was only 14 when she had me and became a young addict herself, so I was raised by my great-grandmother. My grandmother was always working so my great grandmother was the mother of my household. My mother was always a part of my life, but as I said before, I was ashamed of her. When I was pregnant with Son, she was very involved in my life. It was going to be her first grandchild. She even gave me my baby shower, but she didn't live to see his birth. At that time, I went on in life as I normally did, but during this Grief and Loss class and re-enacting the days of my baby shower, her death and Son's birth, I finally broke down. I didn't know how much it had affected me. I thought it had not, but the fact that she didn't get to see her first grandchild was heartbreaking, especially since she threw my baby shower. I cried for days after that, but I was able to release the hurt. My daddy was not very present in my life and his passing didn't affect me much. All I could think of is that he got to meet Son and Mommy didn't. It actually hurt my feelings. That was something else I had to work through.

My Great-Grandmother and Mommy

Another issue I had to deal with was the guilt around my grandfather and his passing. My grandfather had been independent for my whole life. He had a couple of strokes two years before his passing. During those two years, he began falling, starting fires in the elder home apartment he was living in and being very forgetful, so he could no longer live independently. I brought him to live with me, but where I stayed had stairs and he kept going up them while I was at work and falling. I put him in a senior care home in the Lakeview district of San Francisco. They mistreated him so he ran away, and he fell down their cement stairs and broke his hip so he couldn't stay there anymore. He wouldn't let me sue them for the neglect, but I was able to put him in another senior care hospital. When I would go visit him, not very often, he was getting worse and worse. I was just trying to live my life at the time, not knowing how precious that time with him was. I had recently met Mister and those where the good days for us. If I knew what I know now, I would have changed careers to care for my grandfather myself. I've had guilt about it because in that facility, they were stealing his stuff even though it had his name on it, and eventually he couldn't even speak anymore. The last time I went to see him, all he could do was look into my eyes, rub my face and cry. I cried like a baby in his arms. That was not the strong man I grew up with, as he was fragile and it hurt my feelings to see him like that. My last words to him were "Dodo, we will be ok and I don't like seeing you suffer." Little did I know that was the last time he would be alive. I got the call that next morning that he had passed. I felt like I had pardoned him, but wasn't ready for him to go. I just wished I could do it all over. That was another grief I had to get through. In the final days of that class, we had balloons that we tied our grief letters to and let them blow away into the sky. It was a practice to release the grief and it worked.

My grandfather, Dodo

Another benefit I had in the program was to be a leader. I was made head of the kitchen. That meant I was in charge of the menu, the food ordering, the meal prep and the clean-up. I assigned a steady and reliable crew and it kept us all in our right minds. We depended on each other to have a smooth assembly line to serve the entire house of about 300. That was just what I needed: a position of leadership. I learned to cook for the masses and they loved my cooking. I loved the praise and the responsibility of running the kitchen. Sundays were the only day I had off, which I chose to spend at church. Part of my healing process involved forgiving God for all of the tests he put me through, not knowing at the time they were tests of testimony to be shared with others.

The first day I walked back into the church I was raised in, Bethel AME Church in San Francisco, I felt a sense of peace. I was just putting my weight back on and didn't look like the frail person I had become in my addiction. I met with the pastor's wife and the pastor and told them my story. The pastor's wife said, "You should work with our youth ministry." I respectfully declined as I wasn't secure in myself enough to influence others, or so I thought. I also used the excuse that I didn't like kids, Laugh Out Loud. That was God's plan all along, even though I tried to dodge it. I enjoyed going to church on Sundays. I felt my grandmother's presence in the church and I felt right at home. Although I felt at home and at peace in the church, I still asked the question why me Lord? What did I do to deserve all of what I've experienced and lived through? I was at peace with who I was, but not what I had been through. Each visit reminded me of God's grace and His will. The pastor's wife donated a bunch of business suits to the program, but allowed me to pick the ones I wanted first. I was sharp in them suits. As I progressed through the program, it was time for me to leave the kitchen duties and find employment, so that's exactly what I did.

I was in the phase of the program called "re-entry". This is when you've been in the program long enough to be entrusted to live in a shared apartment with other programmers and pay a small rent fee once you find work. Working was mandatory in that part of the program. It was part of the program that focused on responsibilities in the real world, like rent, transportation, etc. My Angel was right there supporting me every step of my journey without being overbearing. He allowed me to do my program successfully without interference. During this time I was also able to go on home passes, which I spent with Son some days and with My Angel on others. When I would visit with Son, he would walk me to the bus stop and stay with me until the bus came, even if it was raining or freezing cold. He was proud of his mommy and his mommy was proud of herself. Having the support of Son and My Angel meant everything to me. I found a good job and got back to the person I knew myself to be.

After nine months in the program, I was able to return home and only had to go to meetings at the program once a week for the next three months. I successfully completed the twelve month program without looking back. I returned home and Son was able to return home with me. At first it was a very rocky start. CPS required us to attend family counseling, which Son hated. It allowed me to talk about that damage I did to him, but I think for him, it brought up memories he didn't want to relive. He was very angry in therapy, but was never angry when I would visit him while I was still in the program. All I could think is that it opened up wounds he didn't want opened. It was during these therapy sessions that I learned he had heard all of the abuse I thought I had concealed while I was with Knight. I never knew he witnessed that, but did know he witnessed the rape and stabbing. He refused to speak about those things and kept them bottled up. I don't think he's ever talked about them. He also didn't like that I was still a strict mother. Since he had not been mothered by me since he was seven and was now twelve, he figured he could say what he wanted to me and treat me how he wanted. WRONG!! I couldn't change what had already been done, but I'll be damned if he was going to disrespect me. I'm from an era of "I brought you into this world and will take you out". He learned the hard way that I meant just that. One day he tried my patience and before I knew it, I had him off the ground by his neck. He learned right then and there that his mama wasn't a joke and was shielding a lot of suppressed anger herself. To this day, our bond is unbreakable.

Giving Back; Beat the Streets, Inc.

In 2004 we moved from the apartment in public housing and I bought my first home. I needed to get Son out of the environment we were in and away from trouble. By this time he had lost his dad to violence and was giving up on living. A year later he lost his brother too and that was the straw that broke the camel's back. My son went into a deep, out of control spiral. His will to live and his faith had been shattered. We moved to Pittsburg, CA to have a change of pace, plus I had an opportunity to be a home owner and jumped on it. When we moved into our home, we noticed an all too familiar situation in the neighborhood. I actually moved him from one environment to the same environment but in a different city. What the hell? I was proud to be a homeowner, but it came with a lot of responsibility. This was my first home and I learned the financial expenses that came along with it were not what I was expecting. I needed to increase my income somehow, legally. My high school friend told me she was getting a pit bull puppy from a litter. I immediately told her I wanted one. Not only did I want it for protection, but also to make some money off of mating him. We named him Smokey. I loved that dog to death. He was very obedient.

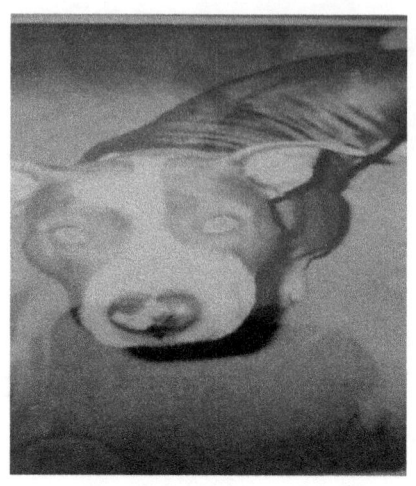

My Smokey

While we were moving into our new home, neighborhood youth helped us move in. They hung out in the neighborhood, acting up. They would out-race each other to cars to sell dope. Not on my watch. I started getting on them about that activity and told them they were bringing down my property value. They soon became friends with Son and I made sure they always had food to eat and somewhere to just come and chill. I wanted them off of the street from hanging out. Every day the youth would be at my house playing video games with Son, and it soon became an expected occurrence. I didn't mind because it kept them out of trouble and I had soon begun school for my master's degree so they kept Son company while I was away. They spent the first Christmas in our new home together with us and our family. They were all good young men, who soon brought cousins, friends, and neighbors with them to chill with us at our house. It was good times.

Little did I know they were acting out while I was gone to work or school. The idiom "While the cat's away, mice will play" is exactly what they did. Since the rape back in 1995, it was common for Son to have friends over instead of going out. I still think it was his way of protecting me, but perhaps he just felt safer at home. I don't know, but I do know that every day there were up to 10 young men in my house. Whatever we ate, they ate. I divided our meal into however many pieces that were needed for everyone to eat. Maybe we didn't get full, but we weren't hungry.

In the process of giving the youth somewhere to be other than running the streets, the police were aware of the ones with criminal records or that they had stopped for whatever reason, so officers began watching my house, and in my opinion, harassing us. To deter their efforts, I created a nonprofit located at my home to allow the young men to come to my house without harassment, and Beat the Streets, Inc. was founded. How fitting of a name, since my efforts were to keep them from running the streets. There were even times that I let them stay with us while in transition. As a mother, I just couldn't leave a youngster on the streets with nowhere to go. I was truly a mom away from home. As in my addiction, I was a strict mom so they got the same rules and direction as Son. I didn't allow disrespecting me, my home, themselves or others in my presence. Of course, that is not how the police saw it. They figured I was aiding the situation, but my intention was to deter the situation. Not long after starting the program, my home was raided. I know we were being targeted because when we first moved in, an officer actually told me "It will not be easy to get rid of you since you own your home". At the time I didn't really pay it any mind, but was aware they were having renters evicted as a nuisance. They knew they could not just call my landlord to complain since I was the owner.

After the raid, I had to leave because the banging on the door and trying to break through it was an all too familiar sound; very similar to the home invasion. By that time, we had gotten another pit bull puppy named Sassy. She was very beautiful. She was the female we would use to mate with Smokey. She even had mating papers, but I really didn't know what that meant. She was just my beautiful baby. During the raid, they removed the dogs and tore everything out of the closets and drawers. Again, very similar to what we experienced in the home invasion, and just like with the home invasion, it was nowhere I wanted to be. They arrested Son and the guys came to help me straighten up the house. The police called me to come get Son, and informed me he would have a court case. I hated that they profiled Son a lot. Even before the raid, they would call me at work stating they had picked him up for being disobedient: Mostly for not telling them his name, not being in school like he was supposed to be and other stuff, but I would always tell them to stop picking him up. Son fit the profile with the long dreads, long white t-shirts and gold teeth, but when you talked to him, you'd find he's very soft spoken. Because he wouldn't talk until he had been taken to the police station, they always called me to come get him. They knew he fit the profile, but didn't meet the actions of the profile. They just wanted to catch him doing whatever they could. They even called me one day saying there was dog fighting at my house, when it was Smokey and Sassy horsing around like they always did. Sassy was an escape artist and often squeezed out of the gate, and Smokey would be right behind her.

My Sassy

After the raid we moved to Antioch and I ended up having the home foreclosed as I couldn't maintain the mortgage on my new house in Antioch and that one in Pittsburg. I never closed Beat the Streets, Inc., just made it by appointment only. Over the years we offered services in education, employment and life skills. All of the services provided came from the requests of the young men and by then young girls too. They would say, "Ms. Tracy, how do I write a resume?" or "Ms. Tracy, I need to get a job, what can I do?" I loved helping them focus on improving themselves. I helped them look for jobs, write resumes, and even helped with homework assignments. For the ones that dropped out of school, I created a scholarship program to offer $250 to those who dropped out but would complete their GED or complete their high school credits to encourage them to complete their education. I also encouraged higher learning, even if starting at a community college. Some did and some didn't. One thing I had to learn with the organization is that even though I wanted to save everyone, everyone can't be saved. I continue to give back to the community through my volunteer services at Beat the Streets, Inc. We moved into our computer center facility in Antioch in 2014 and continue to offer services and resources in education, employment and life skills.

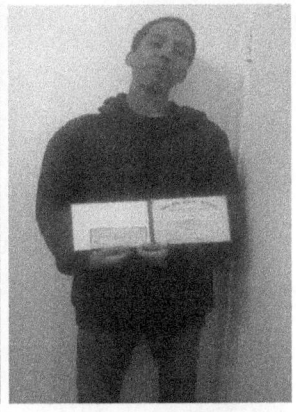

The Triumph

Five Years in a Fog, Overcoming Obstacles depicts the trials and tribulations I endured after a traumatic event in my life. To go from trusting and loving someone wholeheartedly to losing that trust in a blink of an eye is devastating. It's even worse to be followed by one wrong choice after another and then giving up on life. I'm here to tell you that giving up is not about you, but the impact you have on others. I never thought about the impact of the choices I made, not only on myself, but on my son. He has been my rock through it all, even when I was not his rock or protector. No child should have to witness, be a victim of or endure the abuse, neglect and trauma that Son endured. I always tell him, Son you have a story to tell. Although he still does, he allowed me to share part of his story in my story. My son is a strong young man to have endured such actions. As a grown man, he is still my forever love.

One thing I strongly believe is without my foundation of education, I would not have been able to snap back to the life I knew and move forward. I count my blessings that my life wasn't taken, that I'm still standing and that I AM A TRUE SURVIVOR. Not only a survivor of rape, but a survivor of abuse, addiction, and my loss of will to live. I triumphed over it all and stand tall today. I'm standing tall to share my story in an effort to be a blessing to someone who is or has endured abuse in silence like I had. I encourage everyone to talk about your trials and tribulations, but also to turn your mess into a message. Abuse comes in many forms: mental, emotional, and physical. Addiction is not just drugs and drinking, but also includes lying, cheating, stealing, shopping, gambling, and whatever else you can name. Whether it is abuse or addiction, it's hard to fight that battle alone. You suffer in silence when you push people away, like I did. You suffer in silence when you don't talk about your traumatic events, whether with a therapist or someone you trust. The point is you have to release it; otherwise, it is a breeding ground to keep you in bondage. You may not have gone through what I have, but we all have our personal demons, rock bottoms and/or shame we once endured. Talking about it releases the emotions of fear, embarrassment, shame and even denial. One thing is for sure, if you act like something doesn't exist, it doesn't exist to be fixed either. In addiction if you deny that you have a problem, you will never correct it. Who fixes or corrects something that isn't broken? NO ONE. It starts with admission to whatever it is that "doesn't exist". From there it is truly day-by-day, without giving up. What is your "why" to change your life and not be victimized by your circumstances, past events or traumas? Losing Son was mine.

I've been sharing my story with those in a moment of time; however, this is my time to share my story with the masses. I pray that the person reading this can find courage to talk about their trials to release the shame, hurt, embarrassment and any other negative emotions one has when trying to overcome an obstacle. Today I accept my calling to be a mentor and an encouragement to others, young and old. It's never too early or too late to make a change. Many blessings.

About the Author

Tracy L. Tate Jones, a mother, grandmother, wife, CEO, author and speaker, is a native of SF's Bayview District. Having a passion and desire to help the youth in her community and beyond, she started her nonprofit Beat the Streets, Inc. in Pittsburg, CA in 2005 to provide resources in education, employment and life skills to young adults. It was started in order to stop the youth from hanging out on the streets around her home. Welcoming them into her home allowed them to develop a bond that would lead to the services offered today in Antioch, CA. Tracy is also a member of the National Coalition of 100 Black Women, Oakland Chapter as the Chair of the Budget and Finance Committee, which mentors young black girls and provides knowledge to the community on heath and wealth.

Her educational background includes graduating from Lowell High, receiving an AA Degree from Heald Business College, a BA & MBA in Business with an emphasis in Accounting & Public Administration from the University of Phoenix, and a Master's Certificate in Accounting from Keller Graduate School.

Aside from her philanthropic passions, Tracy is also the CEO of TLJ Professional Services, Inc., an accounting professional of over 30 years providing services in bookkeeping, accounting and tax preparation for individuals and small businesses. Tracy is also a life and health insurance provider licensed in CA, NV, TX, IL, KS, GA, MD and MA.

Tracy was motivated to share her story to encourage other women to LIVE life fully. She authored the chapter From the Frying Pan into the Fire in the book compilation, *Broken Into Brilliance Vol. II*. The trials and tribulations she endured are a true testimony of courage, endurance, and a never ending will to live. This was her first book and speaking engagement, but not her last. Tracy counts her blessings to be a blessing to others.

NCBW Induction

Broken Into Brilliance Vol. II.

My Family

www.ingramcontent.com/pod-product-compliance
Lightning Source LLC
Chambersburg PA
CBHW032212040426
42449CB00005B/555